Connect
**With
Text**

What Is a Graphic Novel?

Charlotte Guillain

heinemann
raintree

To contact Capstone Global Library, please call 800-747-4992, or visit our web site
www.capstonepub.com

Edited by Clare Lewis and Holly Beaumont
Designed by Philippa Jenkins
Picture research by Wanda Winch
Originated by Capstone Global Library Ltd
Produced by Helen McCreath
Printed and Bound in China by CTPS

18 17 16 15 14
10 9 8 7 6 5 4 3 2 1

Library of Congress Cataloging-in-Publication Data
Guillain, Charlotte.
  What is a graphic novel? / Charlotte Guillain.
     pages cm.—(Connect with text)
  Includes bibliographical references and index.
   ISBN 978-1-4109-6827-2 (hb)—ISBN 978-1-4109-6833-3 (ebook) 1. Graphic novels—History and criticism—Juvenile literature. 2. Graphic novels—Authorship—Juvenile literature. 3. Comic books, strips, etc.—History and criticism—Juvenile literature. 4. Comic books, strips, etc.—Authorship— Juvenile literature. I. Title.

  PN6710.G85 2015
  741.5'9—dc23   2014016440

This book has been officially leveled by using the F&P Text Level Gradient™ Leveling System.

Acknowledgments
We would like to thank the following for permission to reproduce photographs: ®Batman courtesy of ©DC Comics, 8; Capstone Studio: Karon Dubke, 4, 5, 10, 15, 16, 17, 26, 27, Charles Barnett III and Phil Miller, 21, Daniel Ferran, 11, Dennis Calero, 20, Erik Lervold, 14, Gerardo Sandoval, 7, Jose Alfonso Ocampo Ruiz, 9, Peter McDonnell, 25, Richard Dominguez and Charles Barnett III, 24; Corbis: Reuters/ Benoit Tessier, 22; Getty Images Inc: Gamma-Rapho/Marc Gantier, 19, Mark G. Renders, 18, SFX Magazine/Rob Monk, 12; Newscom: SIPA/Saez Pascal, 6; Rex USA: c.Goldwyn/Everett, 13; Shutterstock: deedl, 23, solarseven, cover (bottom right), urfin, pencil.

Contents

Have You Ever Read a Graphic Novel? ... 4

What Is a Graphic Novel? 6

Characters.. 8

Plot 10

Words and Pictures............................... 12

The Tools of the Trade 14

Making a Graphic Novel...................... 16

Ligne Claire–Style Graphic Novels 18

Comic Book–Style Graphic Novels 20

Other Styles of Graphic Novel............ 22

Graphic Nonfiction 24

Finding the Right Graphic Novel
    for You... 26

Take It Further....................................... 28

Glossary 30

Find Out More 31

Index..32

Some words are shown in bold, **like this**.
You can find out what they mean by
looking in the glossary.

Have You Ever Read a Graphic Novel?

What do you like to read? Most of us start out reading picture books. In the best picture books, the illustrations tell us more about the story than the words alone. Graphic novels also combine the storytelling power of pictures and words in an amazing way. When you read one, you look at the illustrations for clues about the story while you read the words spoken by the characters.

You can enjoy many picture books at any age.

Reading a graphic novel is a very different experience than reading an ordinary novel, and it can be very exciting. If you like comics, you will probably enjoy graphic novels. If you have never read any books like this, then give one a try. This book will give you lots of ideas to get you started.

see for yourself

Find some picture books in the library or on your bookshelves. Look carefully at the illustrations. Can you spot information in the pictures as well as the words? Now that you are older, can you see more to the story than a younger child would?

What Is a Graphic Novel?

A graphic novel is different than comics and other books in several ways. The main feature of a graphic novel is that it is a complete story made up of words and pictures, and it is drawn in a comic strip **format**. Stories in comics are often published in weekly **episodes**—so you may have to wait to find out what happens next! Sometimes lots of comic strip episodes are put together to make a graphic novel.

Famous fiction

The writer Neil Gaiman has written stories for comic books, such as *The Sandman*. Originally, the stories were published in monthly episodes by DC Comics. They were so popular that the episodes were later collected together and published as a complete graphic novel.

Neil Gaiman has written many different types of book, including graphic novels.

In graphic novels, the characters' speech and thoughts are set in speech bubbles. This means you won't see quotation marks, like you would in an ordinary novel.

A graphic novel can be fiction or nonfiction. Many graphic novels tell fantastical stories. Others are **biographies** or tell the reader about real historical events.

Quotation marks aren't used in a graphic novel.

Characters

The characters are the people we get to know as a story unfolds. In ordinary novels, writers need to describe their characters so we know what they look like and how they behave. In a graphic novel, the writer doesn't need to describe the characters because the pictures show all their **features**. In fact, a graphic novel can tell us a lot more about characters in just a glance.

BATMAN © DC Comics

Famous fiction

The character Batman was created in 1939 by illustrator Bob Kane. Stories about Batman were published by DC Comics and became very popular. Today, Batman is also a well-known character in movies and on television.

In a graphic novel, there is usually a main hero, or **protagonist**. These characters normally want something and have to overcome challenges to achieve their goals. There are also other characters who help the heroes—and villains who try to stop them. It's important that all the characters look different from each other because the reader won't be told who is speaking, as in an ordinary novel. We have to recognize who is speaking by looking at each illustration.

Many of the best stories are about a battle between good and evil.

Plot

Like all stories, a graphic novel needs to have a gripping **plot** to keep the reader turning the page. Lots of stories start with an exciting opening, followed by a series of events where the hero is trying to get what he or she wants. There is often a twist at the end to surprise the reader!

Many writers spend a lot of time planning the plots of their stories.

Long-lost cousin arrives

Enter new character

The necklace is missing

Alarms go off

Fight in the library

Plot twist?

Sees someone moving around in the dark

Tapping

Finds clues in old photos

Mysterious phone call

Chase through the dark

Meets an old rival...

She goes home to find...

Famous fiction

Graphic novels that were first published as stories in comics would have come in weekly or monthly installments. Each **episode** would usually end on a cliffhanger moment to make the reader want to buy the next edition. When these installments are put together to make a graphic novel, it can make an exciting plot that is full of tense moments.

The plot in a graphic novel is often shorter than in an ordinary novel. This is because the images that tell so much of the story take up a lot of space and show detailed scenes on every spread.

Pictures can tell much of the plot without any words at all.

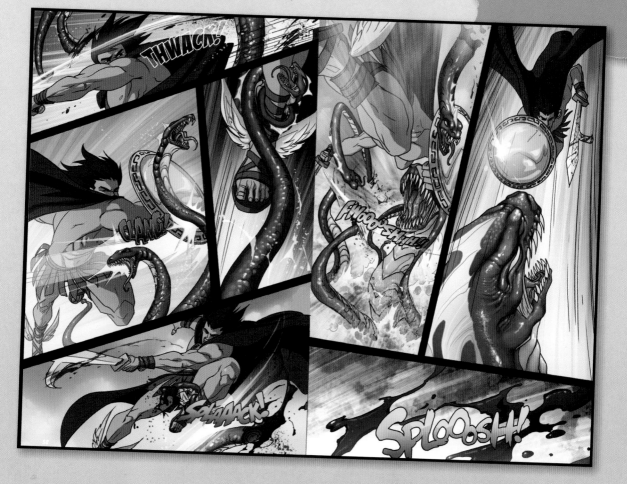

Words and Pictures

With some graphic novels, the same person comes up with the story and draws the pictures. With others, one person writes the words and another person illustrates them. The writer might work with the illustrator as he or she develops the story, so they both have ideas about the finished text. The pictures can show all sorts of information that there wouldn't be space to describe in words. An illustration can also have a much greater impact than a lot of text.

Famous fiction

Dave Gibbons is a British artist who is well known for his illustrations of superheroes in comic books and graphic novels. He has created the images for stories about Doctor Who, Green Lantern, and Watchmen. The *Watchmen* graphic novel, illustrated by Gibbons, is one of the best-selling graphic novels.

Neil Gaiman has worked closely with the illustrator Dave McKean on several of his books.

Another benefit of reading graphic novels is that if you sometimes come across words that you haven't seen before, the pictures might help you to understand what they mean without having to reach for a dictionary!

The Tools of the Trade

Traditionally, people who write and illustrate graphic novels start with a pencil and paper. They produce many sketches as they develop each character and give them a distinctive look. Today, some graphic novel creators draw straight onto a computer. Others sketch out their pictures in pencil first and then scan them in. Special computer software can make the illustrations sharper and more finished, and then the illustrator can add color.

Sketching with a pencil is a good way to figure out what characters should look like.

Illustrators need to have all the right tools before they can start work.

The most important tools a graphic novel writer and artist needs are:

- plenty of paper
- a ruler
- a pencil
- an eraser
- a thin black drawing pen
- colored pencils, pens, or inks.

Write your own

Make sure you start with a very soft pencil. You will need to make your drawings very light so that you can easily erase the pencil marks after you have gone over them in pen.

Making a Graphic Novel

Graphic novel writers start by planning out their story. They need a strong **plot** and different characters. The illustrator makes lots of sketches of each character to show what clothes and belongings they have.

Next, they make rough plans to show which part of the story will be told on each page. This is called a **storyboard**. They mark out boxes that show each stage in the story sequence and make rough sketches of what will happen in each box.

The storyboard starts as a rough sketch so it's easy to make changes.

Write your own

The last picture on each right-hand page of a graphic novel is important. It's good to show an exciting moment here, so the reader can't wait to turn the page and see what happens next. There might be a question or a joke there, so the reader has to turn the page to find the answer or **punch line!**

Then, the illustrator gradually adds more and more detail.

When they have drawn a storyboard, they make the pictures more detailed using a soft pencil before going over them in pen. Then, they add color. It's important to leave enough room in each panel for all the words in speech bubbles and boxes!

Ligne Claire–Style Graphic Novels

The illustrations in graphic novels can be drawn in different styles. The artwork style used in the *Tintin* books by the Belgian writer and illustrator Hergé is called **ligne claire**. This means "clear line" in French. It has this name because all the strong, black outlines in the drawing are the same thickness. The illustrator doesn't use different widths of line to show parts of the picture that are near, or far, or in shadow. Bold blocks of color are used rather than complicated **shading**. This style has a very clear and simple effect.

Hergé's *Tintin* books have been translated into many different languages.

Hergé produced *Tintin* books until he died in 1983.

Hergé was one of the first illustrators to use this drawing style in the 1940s. During World War II, it was impossible to import comic books from the United States, so European artists developed their own, quite different style.

Famous fiction

Garen Ewing wrote and illustrated the *Rainbow Orchid* books. These graphic novels are about the adventures of a young historical researcher named Julius Chancer. Ewing started creating these stories in the 1990s, but the *ligne claire* style perfectly suits his stories, which are set in the 1920s.

Comic Book–Style Graphic Novels

American comic books started to become popular in the late 1930s and during the 1940s. The stories were often about superheroes, such as Spider-Man, Superman, and Batman. The illustrations usually include lots of detail, and the artists draw lines of different thickness to create depth and shade. They often use a technique called **cross-hatching** and sometimes use blocks of black ink to create a bold, striking effect.

Cross-hatching is where lines are layered in different directions to add **shading**.

This comic book style is used in many graphic novels today. Illustrators show some scenes very close up or from unusual angles, and they can show a lot of movement. The characters often have very exaggerated **features**—for example, huge muscles and chiseled faces.

SCREECH!!

Metal tore as the iceberg ripped through the hull. Instantly, thousands of gallons of water poured into the lower areas of the ship.

Famous fiction

Writer Jerry Siegel and illustrator Joe Shuster were still in school when they created the character of Superman in the 1930s. A few years later, it was bought by the company now known as DC Comics. Since then, Superman has starred in many graphic novels as well as movies, cartoons, comic books, and television series.

Sometimes text is used as part of the artwork to create sound effects.

Other Styles of Graphic Novel

Many other drawing styles are used in graphic novels. Some illustrators use a very cartoony style—for example, in the *Asterix* books by René Goscinny and Albert Uderzo. The characters started out as a serial comic strip in a French magazine, but they went on to star in many hilarious graphic novels, cartoons, and movies.

The *Asterix* graphic novels have been translated into many languages.

The **manga** style of artwork developed in Japan and has become very popular across the world. Manga stories tend to follow themes, such as romance, adventure, magic, or school life. A manga-style graphic novel can be hundreds of pages long.

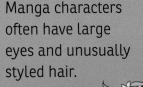

Manga characters often have large eyes and unusually styled hair.

Famous fiction

Many graphic novels for children are produced by children's picture book illustrators. Raymond Briggs writes and illustrates stories such as *The Snowman* and *Fungus the Bogeyman*. These are sold as picture books, but they are really graphic novels. Shaun Tan's *The Arrival* could be described as a wordless graphic novel. Illustrators such as Sarah McIntyre illustrate picture books and children's novels in addition to creating comics and graphic novels.

Graphic Nonfiction

Graphic novels are not just a great way to tell a fictional story. The unique combination of words and images is also a great way to describe all sorts of nonfiction subjects. Many graphic novelists have told their own **autobiography** or another person's **biography** using this type of text.

Graphic nonfiction can explain complex ideas in a clear, visual way.

Subjects such as science and history can also be described and explained using a graphic novel **format**. The illustrations can help to explain difficult ideas in a clearer way. Historical events can be brought to life, with clothing and **artifacts** shown in detail.

Graphic nonfiction can make stories from history interesting and exciting.

Write your own

Why not try writing an extract from your own autobiography in a graphic novel style? Choose an event from your life that you want to share. Who was involved? Draw the different "characters." Then, work up a rough **storyboard** to show what happened.

Finding the Right Graphic Novel for You

If you've never read a graphic novel, are you wondering where to start? If you read a comic, maybe some of the writers and illustrators have also produced graphic novels. For example, Jamie Smart has written and illustrated comic strips in *The Phoenix* comic and has also published the graphic novel *Fish-Head Steve*.

You may find graphic novels about characters you have seen in movies or on television.

You could look at the comic's web site or look up the writers' and illustrators' own web sites to find out what else they have created.

You could also ask your librarian, local bookseller, or teacher to recommend a graphic novel. If you normally like adventure books, prefer funny books, or always read mystery stories, then there will probably be a graphic novel that is right for you. If you've read a good graphic novel, lend it to a friend and see what he or she thinks. Can your friends suggest any graphic novels that they have enjoyed reading?

If your friends read graphic novels, ask them for some recommendations.

see for yourself

Visit one of the web sites at the back of this book and search for graphic novels for children your age. Has anyone written a review of the books? Why not borrow one from your library and see what it's like?

Take It Further...

Do you want to create your own graphic novel? Here are some ways to get started:

1. Read as many comics and graphic novels as you can. Think about how the story is told using the pictures as much as the words.

2. Look at different artwork styles and decide if you want to try to draw in one of those styles. Try copying the way some of the characters have been drawn.

3. Come up with a good story. Make sure you include some good twists!

4. Draw sketches of all the characters in your story. Do they all look and behave differently enough to prevent the reader from getting confused?

5. Sketch out a **storyboard**, making sure you show all the important stages of the story. You could make some panels extra big if you want these sections to stand out.

6. Draw each panel in more detail with a soft pencil, including your speech bubbles and text boxes. Then, go over the top with a black drawing pen. After you have erased the pencil lines, add color and write the speech bubbles and other words.

Ideas to get you started

An evil genius is threatening to drain all the water out of the city and force the people who live there to work as his slaves. Only one hero can save the day...

A schoolgirl has magical powers that she uses to try to help people. But sometimes her good ideas backfire!

Thieves have stolen a priceless carving from the museum. Nobody knows where the thieves are, but they have left some important clues behind. Who can solve the clues and track the carving down?

Glossary

artifact object made by humans

autobiography writer's own life story

biography someone else's life story

cross-hatching lines drawn over each other at different angles

episode one section of a longer story

feature part of a person or thing that stands out

format style or layout of something

ligne claire style of graphic novel illustration that has clear black outlines

manga style of graphic novel illustration that started in Japan

plot storyline

protagonist main character

punch line final line of a joke

shading adding of light and dark to a drawing

storyboard sequence of sketches that show what will happen, and where, in a graphic novel

Find Out More

Books

Coope, Katy. *How to Draw Manga*. New York: Tangerine, 2003.

Hamilton, John. *Graphic Novel* (You Write It!). Edina, Minn.: ABDO, 2009.

Lee, Frank. *How to Draw Your Own Graphic Novel*. New York: PowerKids, 2012.

Milbourne, Anna. *Drawing Cartoons* (Usborne Art Ideas). Tulsa, Okla.: EDC, 2003.

Rosinsky, Natalie M. *Graphic Novel* (Write Your Own). Minneapolis: Compass Point, 2009.

Web sites

FactHound offers a safe, fun way to find Internet sites related to this book. All of the sites on FactHound have been researched by our staff.

Here's all you do:
Visit www.facthound.com
Type in this code: 9781410968272

Index

artwork styles 18–23, 28
Asterix 22
autobiographies and biographies 7, 24, 25

Batman 8, 20
Briggs, Raymond 23

cartoon style 22
characters 8–9, 16, 21
comic book style 20–21
comic strip format 6, 22
comics 5, 6, 11, 26
computer software 14
creating your own graphic novel 15, 16–17, 25, 28–29
cross-hatching 20

episodes 6, 11
Ewing, Garen 19
exaggerated features 21

fiction 7
finding graphic novels to read 5, 26–27

Gaiman, Neil 6, 13
Gibbons, Dave 12
graphic novel, definition 6–7

Hergé 18, 19
heroes 9, 10

illustrations 4, 6, 8, 11, 12–13, 14, 17, 18, 20–21

libraries 5, 27
ligne claire style 18–19

McKean, Dave 13
manga style 23

nonfiction 7, 24–25
novels 7, 8

picture books 4, 23
plots 10–11, 16
protagonists 9
punch lines 17

Shuster, Joe 21
Siegel, Jerry 21
sketching 14, 15, 16, 28
Smart, Jamie 26
sound effects 21
speech bubbles 7, 17, 29
storyboards 16, 17, 25, 28
Superman 20, 21

tense moments 11
tools 14–15
twists 10, 28

villains 9

Watchmen 12
words 12, 13